THIS JOURNAL BELONGS TO:

_____

OnWithYourLife.com

Published by:
POWER HOUSE
AN IMPRINT OF POWER HOUSE STUDIOS LLC
thepowerhousestudio.com

ISBN# 979-8-9853756-2-6 (Paperback) ISBN# 979-8-9853756-3-3 (eBook)
ISBN# 979-8-9853756-8-8 (Workbook) ISBN# 979-8-9853756-7-1 (Journal)

Welcome to your next steps as you move on with your life!

This is what the Lord, the God of Israel says:
"Write all the words which I have spoken to you in a book."
(Jeremiah 30:2 NASB)

This journal was designed to be a stand-alone journal. You will find it helpful to use daily as you move forward and get on with your life.

It can also be a great help when used with our other available tools, including the book entitled, *OFF the Merry-Go-Round and ON with Your Life!* by Dana Marie Ecklund and its companion workbook. All of these tools are available at

ONWITHYOURLIFE.COM

If you purchased this journal to use with the book, we encourage you to write in your journal as you read through the book. Here are some suggestions:

- Date each journal entry and complete one section for every chapter.

- Write down your thoughts and emotions as you read.

- Write down your "AHA!" moments.
  (These are things you have never heard before, or perhaps you have previously heard but now they are striking you as life-changing.)

- Write down things you have questions about.

- Write down things you recognize you need to change in your life.

- Write down what you know God is saying to you as you read.

- Write down scriptures that you want to meditate on.

- Write down stories of your own life that come to mind.

These journal entries will help you get on your God-provided path in life. After reading the book and taking notes in your journal, start using the coordinating workbook immediately. Use your journal entries to help you remember your thoughts and questions as you walk through your own process and path to victory in the workbook.

CONGRATULATIONS! YOU HAVE TAKEN YOUR FIRST STEPS IN THE PROCESS TO GET OFF THE MERRY-GO-ROUND AND ON WITH YOUR LIFE!

DATE: _____

JOURNALING - THOUGHTS, EMOTIONS, AND
SCRIPTURES TO THINK ON. WHAT DID GOD
SAY TO ME TODAY? _____

_____

_____

_____

_____

_____

_____

_____

_____

_____

ON WITH YOUR life

TOP 3 GOOD THINGS TODAY:
○ _____
○ _____
○ _____

TOP 3 AREAS THAT NEED CHANGE:
○ _____
○ _____
○ _____

HOW WOULD YOU RATE THE DAY?
☆ ☆ ☆ ☆ ☆

WHAT I AM READING TODAY:

QUESTIONS I HAVE TODAY:
○ _____
○ _____
○ _____

DATE: _____

"AHA!" MOMENTS (THINGS I NEVER HEARD
BEFORE OR THAT STRUCK ME AS LIFE-
CHANGING). WHAT DID I LEARN TODAY?
WHAT AM I GRATEFUL FOR TODAY?

ON
WITH YOUR
life

_____

_____

_____

_____

_____

_____

_____

_____

_____

_____

_____

_____

_____

_____

_____

_____

_____

_____

_____

_____

Dreams, Visions, and Life Goals

Date:

Topic:

Record Special Thoughts on Your Dreams, Visions, and Life Goals
(You can write, doodle, or paste pictures of vision list items.)

DATE: _____

JOURNALING - THOUGHTS, EMOTIONS, AND
SCRIPTURES TO THINK ON. WHAT DID GOD
SAY TO ME TODAY? _____

_____

_____

_____

_____

_____

_____

_____

_____

_____

_____

TOP 3 GOOD THINGS TODAY: _____

○ _____

○ _____

○ _____

WHAT I AM READING TODAY: _____

TOP 3 AREAS THAT NEED CHANGE:

○ _____

○ _____

○ _____

QUESTIONS I HAVE TODAY: _____

○ _____

HOW WOULD YOU RATE THE DAY?

☆ ☆ ☆ ☆ ☆

○ _____

○ _____

DATE: _____

"AHA!" MOMENTS (THINGS I NEVER HEARD
BEFORE OR THAT STRUCK ME AS LIFE-
CHANGING). WHAT DID I LEARN TODAY?
WHAT AM I GRATEFUL FOR TODAY?

**ON
WITH YOUR
life**

_____

_____

_____

_____

_____

_____

_____

_____

_____

_____

_____

_____

_____

_____

_____

_____

_____

_____

_____

_____

_____

Dreams, Visions, and Life Goals

Date:

Topic:

Record Special Thoughts on Your Dreams, Visions, and Life Goals
(You can write, doodle, or paste pictures of vision list items.)

DATE: _____

JOURNALING - THOUGHTS, EMOTIONS, AND
SCRIPTURES TO THINK ON. WHAT DID GOD
SAY TO ME TODAY? _____

_____

_____

_____

_____

_____

_____

_____

_____

_____

_____

TOP 3 GOOD THINGS TODAY:
○ _____
○ _____
○ _____

TOP 3 AREAS THAT NEED CHANGE:
○ _____
○ _____
○ _____

HOW WOULD YOU RATE THE DAY?
☆ ☆ ☆ ☆ ☆

WHAT I AM READING TODAY:

QUESTIONS I HAVE TODAY:
○ _____
○ _____
○ _____

ON
WITH YOUR
life

DATE: _____

"AHA!" MOMENTS (THINGS I NEVER HEARD
BEFORE OR THAT STRUCK ME AS LIFE-
CHANGING). WHAT DID I LEARN TODAY?
WHAT AM I GRATEFUL FOR TODAY?

ON
WITH YOUR
life

_____

_____

_____

_____

_____

_____

_____

_____

_____

_____

_____

_____

_____

_____

_____

_____

_____

_____

_____

Dreams, Visions, and Life Goals

Date:

Topic:

Record Special Thoughts on Your Dreams, Visions, and Life Goals
(You can write, doodle, or paste pictures of vision list items.)

DATE: _____

JOURNALING - THOUGHTS, EMOTIONS, AND
SCRIPTURES TO THINK ON. WHAT DID GOD
SAY TO ME TODAY? _____

ON
WITH YOUR
life

_____

_____

_____

_____

_____

_____

_____

_____

_____

_____

TOP 3 GOOD THINGS TODAY:
○ _____

○ _____

○ _____

WHAT I AM READING TODAY:

TOP 3 AREAS THAT NEED CHANGE:
○ _____

○ _____

○ _____

QUESTIONS I HAVE TODAY:
○ _____

HOW WOULD YOU RATE THE DAY?
☆ ☆ ☆ ☆ ☆

○ _____

○ _____

DATE: _____

"AHA!" MOMENTS (THINGS I NEVER HEARD
BEFORE OR THAT STRUCK ME AS LIFE-
CHANGING). WHAT DID I LEARN TODAY?
WHAT AM I GRATEFUL FOR TODAY?

ON
WITH YOUR
life

_____

_____

_____

_____

_____

_____

_____

_____

_____

_____

_____

_____

_____

_____

_____

_____

_____

_____

_____

_____

_____

_____

Dreams, Visions, and Life Goals

Date:

Topic:

Record Special Thoughts on Your Dreams, Visions, and Life Goals
(You can write, doodle, or paste pictures of vision list items.)

DATE: _____

JOURNALING - THOUGHTS, EMOTIONS, AND
SCRIPTURES TO THINK ON. WHAT DID GOD
SAY TO ME TODAY? _____

_____

_____

_____

_____

_____

_____

_____

_____

_____

_____

ON WITH YOUR life

TOP 3 GOOD THINGS TODAY:
○ _____
○ _____
○ _____

TOP 3 AREAS THAT NEED CHANGE:
○ _____
○ _____
○ _____

HOW WOULD YOU RATE THE DAY?
☆ ☆ ☆ ☆ ☆

WHAT I AM READING TODAY:

QUESTIONS I HAVE TODAY:
○ _____
○ _____
○ _____

DATE: _____

"AHA!" MOMENTS (THINGS I NEVER HEARD
BEFORE OR THAT STRUCK ME AS LIFE-
CHANGING). WHAT DID I LEARN TODAY?
WHAT AM I GRATEFUL FOR TODAY?

ON
WITH YOUR
life

_____

_____

_____

_____

_____

_____

_____

_____

_____

_____

_____

_____

_____

_____

_____

_____

_____

_____

_____

_____

_____

_____

Dreams, Visions, and Life Goals

Date:

Topic:

Record Special Thoughts on Your Dreams, Visions, and Life Goals
(You can write, doodle, or paste pictures of vision list items.)

DATE: _____

JOURNALING - THOUGHTS, EMOTIONS, AND
SCRIPTURES TO THINK ON. WHAT DID GOD
SAY TO ME TODAY? _____

_____

_____

_____

_____

_____

_____

_____

_____

_____

ON WITH YOUR life

TOP 3 GOOD THINGS TODAY: _____

○ _____

○ _____

○ _____

WHAT I AM READING TODAY: _____

TOP 3 AREAS THAT NEED CHANGE: ____

○ _____

○ _____

○ _____

QUESTIONS I HAVE TODAY: _____

○ _____

HOW WOULD YOU RATE THE DAY?

☆ ☆ ☆ ☆ ☆

○ _____

○ _____

DATE: _____

"AHA!" MOMENTS (THINGS I NEVER HEARD
BEFORE OR THAT STRUCK ME AS LIFE-
CHANGING). WHAT DID I LEARN TODAY?
WHAT AM I GRATEFUL FOR TODAY?

ON
WITH YOUR
life

_____

_____

_____

_____

_____

_____

_____

_____

_____

_____

_____

_____

_____

_____

_____

_____

_____

_____

_____

_____

_____

_____

Dreams, Visions, and Life Goals

Date:

Topic:

Record Special Thoughts on Your Dreams, Visions, and Life Goals
(You can write, doodle, or paste pictures of vision list items.)

DATE: _____

JOURNALING - THOUGHTS, EMOTIONS, AND
SCRIPTURES TO THINK ON. WHAT DID GOD
SAY TO ME TODAY? _____

_____

_____

_____

_____

_____

_____

_____

_____

_____

ON
WITH YOUR
life

TOP 3 GOOD THINGS TODAY:
○ _____
○ _____
○ _____

WHAT I AM READING TODAY:

TOP 3 AREAS THAT NEED CHANGE:
○ _____
○ _____
○ _____

QUESTIONS I HAVE TODAY:
○ _____
○ _____
○ _____

HOW WOULD YOU RATE THE DAY?
☆ ☆ ☆ ☆ ☆

DATE: _____

"AHA!" MOMENTS (THINGS I NEVER HEARD
BEFORE OR THAT STRUCK ME AS LIFE-
CHANGING). WHAT DID I LEARN TODAY?
WHAT AM I GRATEFUL FOR TODAY?

ON
WITH YOUR
life

Dreams, Visions, and Life Goals

Date:

Topic:

Record Special Thoughts on Your Dreams, Visions, and Life Goals
(You can write, doodle, or paste pictures of vision list items.)

DATE: _____

JOURNALING - THOUGHTS, EMOTIONS, AND
SCRIPTURES TO THINK ON. WHAT DID GOD
SAY TO ME TODAY? _____

_____

_____

_____

_____

_____

_____

_____

_____

_____

TOP 3 GOOD THINGS TODAY: _____
○ _____
○ _____
○ _____

WHAT I AM READING TODAY:

TOP 3 AREAS THAT NEED CHANGE:
○ _____
○ _____
○ _____

QUESTIONS I HAVE TODAY: _____
○ _____
○ _____

HOW WOULD YOU RATE THE DAY?
☆ ☆ ☆ ☆ ☆
○ _____

DATE: _____

"AHA!" MOMENTS (THINGS I NEVER HEARD
BEFORE OR THAT STRUCK ME AS LIFE-
CHANGING). WHAT DID I LEARN TODAY?
WHAT AM I GRATEFUL FOR TODAY?

ON
WITH YOUR
life

_____

_____

_____

_____

_____

_____

_____

_____

_____

_____

_____

_____

_____

_____

_____

_____

_____

_____

_____

_____

Dreams, Visions, and Life Goals

Date:

Topic:

Record Special Thoughts on Your Dreams, Visions, and Life Goals
(You can write, doodle, or paste pictures of vision list items.)

DATE: _____

JOURNALING - THOUGHTS, EMOTIONS, AND
SCRIPTURES TO THINK ON. WHAT DID GOD
SAY TO ME TODAY? _____

_____

_____

_____

_____

_____

_____

_____

_____

_____

TOP 3 GOOD THINGS TODAY: _____

○ _____

○ _____

○ _____

TOP 3 AREAS THAT NEED CHANGE:

○ _____

○ _____

○ _____

HOW WOULD YOU RATE THE DAY? _____

☆ ☆ ☆ ☆ ☆

WHAT I AM READING TODAY: _____

QUESTIONS I HAVE TODAY: _____

○ _____

○ _____

○ _____

DATE: _____

"AHA!" MOMENTS (THINGS I NEVER HEARD
BEFORE OR THAT STRUCK ME AS LIFE-
CHANGING). WHAT DID I LEARN TODAY?
WHAT AM I GRATEFUL FOR TODAY?

ON
WITH YOUR
life

_____

_____

_____

_____

_____

_____

_____

_____

_____

_____

_____

_____

_____

_____

_____

_____

_____

_____

_____

_____

_____

Dreams, Visions, and Life Goals

Date:

Topic:

Record Special Thoughts on Your Dreams, Visions, and Life Goals
(You can write, doodle, or paste pictures of vision list items.)

DATE: _____

JOURNALING - THOUGHTS, EMOTIONS, AND
SCRIPTURES TO THINK ON. WHAT DID GOD
SAY TO ME TODAY? _____

_____

_____

_____

_____

_____

_____

_____

_____

_____

ON WITH YOUR life

TOP 3 GOOD THINGS TODAY:
○ _____

○ _____

○ _____

TOP 3 AREAS THAT NEED CHANGE:
○ _____

○ _____

○ _____

HOW WOULD YOU RATE THE DAY?
☆ ☆ ☆ ☆ ☆

WHAT I AM READING TODAY:

QUESTIONS I HAVE TODAY:
○ _____

○ _____

○ _____

DATE: _____

"AHA!" MOMENTS (THINGS I NEVER HEARD
BEFORE OR THAT STRUCK ME AS LIFE-
CHANGING). WHAT DID I LEARN TODAY?
WHAT AM I GRATEFUL FOR TODAY?

ON
WITH YOUR
life

Dreams, Visions, and Life Goals

Date:

Topic:

Record Special Thoughts on Your Dreams, Visions, and Life Goals
(You can write, doodle, or paste pictures of vision list items.)

DATE: _____

JOURNALING - THOUGHTS, EMOTIONS, AND
SCRIPTURES TO THINK ON. WHAT DID GOD
SAY TO ME TODAY?

_____

_____
_____
_____
_____
_____
_____
_____
_____
_____
_____

ON WITH YOUR life

TOP 3 GOOD THINGS TODAY:
○ _____
○ _____
○ _____

TOP 3 AREAS THAT NEED CHANGE:
○ _____
○ _____
○ _____

HOW WOULD YOU RATE THE DAY?
☆ ☆ ☆ ☆ ☆

WHAT I AM READING TODAY:

QUESTIONS I HAVE TODAY:
○ _____
○ _____
○ _____

DATE: _____

"AHA!" MOMENTS (THINGS I NEVER HEARD
BEFORE OR THAT STRUCK ME AS LIFE-
CHANGING). WHAT DID I LEARN TODAY?
WHAT AM I GRATEFUL FOR TODAY?

ON
WITH YOUR
life

_____

_____

_____

_____

_____

_____

_____

_____

_____

_____

_____

_____

_____

_____

_____

_____

_____

_____

_____

_____

_____

_____

Dreams, Visions, and Life Goals

Date:

Topic:

Record Special Thoughts on Your Dreams, Visions, and Life Goals
(You can write, doodle, or paste pictures of vision list items.)

DATE: _____

JOURNALING - THOUGHTS, EMOTIONS, AND
SCRIPTURES TO THINK ON. WHAT DID GOD
SAY TO ME TODAY? _____

ON
WITH YOUR
life

_____
_____
_____
_____
_____
_____
_____
_____
_____

TOP 3 GOOD THINGS TODAY:
○ _____
○ _____
○ _____

WHAT I AM READING TODAY: _____

TOP 3 AREAS THAT NEED CHANGE:
○ _____
○ _____
○ _____

QUESTIONS I HAVE TODAY: _____
○ _____

HOW WOULD YOU RATE THE DAY?
☆ ☆ ☆ ☆ ☆
○ _____
○ _____

DATE: _____

"AHA!" MOMENTS (THINGS I NEVER HEARD
BEFORE OR THAT STRUCK ME AS LIFE-
CHANGING). WHAT DID I LEARN TODAY?
WHAT AM I GRATEFUL FOR TODAY?

ON
WITH YOUR
life

_____

_____

_____

_____

_____

_____

_____

_____

_____

_____

_____

_____

_____

_____

_____

_____

_____

_____

_____

_____

_____

Dreams, Visions, and Life Goals

Date:

Topic:

Record Special Thoughts on Your Dreams, Visions, and Life Goals
(You can write, doodle, or paste pictures of vision list items.)

DATE: _____

JOURNALING - THOUGHTS, EMOTIONS, AND
SCRIPTURES TO THINK ON. WHAT DID GOD
SAY TO ME TODAY?

_____

_____

_____

_____

_____

_____

_____

_____

_____

_____

TOP 3 GOOD THINGS TODAY:
○ _____
○ _____
○ _____

TOP 3 AREAS THAT NEED CHANGE:
○ _____
○ _____
○ _____

HOW WOULD YOU RATE THE DAY?
☆ ☆ ☆ ☆ ☆

WHAT I AM READING TODAY:

QUESTIONS I HAVE TODAY:
○ _____
○ _____
○ _____

DATE: _____

"AHA!" MOMENTS (THINGS I NEVER HEARD
BEFORE OR THAT STRUCK ME AS LIFE-
CHANGING). WHAT DID I LEARN TODAY?
WHAT AM I GRATEFUL FOR TODAY?

ON
WITH YOUR
life

_____

_____

_____

_____

_____

_____

_____

_____

_____

_____

_____

_____

_____

_____

_____

_____

_____

_____

_____

_____

_____

Dreams, Visions, and Life Goals

Date:

Topic:

Record Special Thoughts on Your Dreams, Visions, and Life Goals
(You can write, doodle, or paste pictures of vision list items.)

DATE: _____

JOURNALING - THOUGHTS, EMOTIONS, AND
SCRIPTURES TO THINK ON. WHAT DID GOD
SAY TO ME TODAY? _____

_____

_____

_____

_____

_____

_____

_____

_____

_____

_____

TOP 3 GOOD THINGS TODAY: _____

○ _____

○ _____

○ _____

WHAT I AM READING TODAY: _____

TOP 3 AREAS THAT NEED CHANGE:

○ _____

○ _____

○ _____

QUESTIONS I HAVE TODAY: _____

○ _____

HOW WOULD YOU RATE THE DAY?

☆ ☆ ☆ ☆ ☆

○ _____

○ _____

ON WITH YOUR life

DATE: _____

'AHA!" MOMENTS (THINGS I NEVER HEARD
BEFORE OR THAT STRUCK ME AS LIFE-
CHANGING). WHAT DID I LEARN TODAY?
WHAT AM I GRATEFUL FOR TODAY?

ON
WITH YOUR
life

Dreams, Visions, and Life Goals

Date:

Topic:

Record Special Thoughts on Your Dreams, Visions, and Life Goals
(You can write, doodle, or paste pictures of vision list items.)

DATE: _____

JOURNALING - THOUGHTS, EMOTIONS, AND
SCRIPTURES TO THINK ON. WHAT DID GOD
SAY TO ME TODAY?

_____

_____

_____

_____

_____

_____

_____

_____

_____

_____

TOP 3 GOOD THINGS TODAY:
○ _____

○ _____

○ _____

TOP 3 AREAS THAT NEED CHANGE:
○ _____

○ _____

○ _____

HOW WOULD YOU RATE THE DAY?
☆ ☆ ☆ ☆ ☆

WHAT I AM READING TODAY:

QUESTIONS I HAVE TODAY:
○ _____

○ _____

○ _____

DATE: _____

"AHA!" MOMENTS (THINGS I NEVER HEARD
BEFORE OR THAT STRUCK ME AS LIFE-
CHANGING). WHAT DID I LEARN TODAY?
WHAT AM I GRATEFUL FOR TODAY?

ON
WITH YOUR
life

_____

_____

_____

_____

_____

_____

_____

_____

_____

_____

_____

_____

_____

_____

_____

_____

_____

_____

_____

_____

_____

Dreams, Visions, and Life Goals

Date:

Topic:

Record Special Thoughts on Your Dreams, Visions, and Life Goals
(You can write, doodle, or paste pictures of vision list items.)

DATE: _____

JOURNALING - THOUGHTS, EMOTIONS, AND
SCRIPTURES TO THINK ON. WHAT DID GOD
SAY TO ME TODAY? _____

_____

_____

_____

_____

_____

_____

_____

_____

_____

TOP 3 GOOD THINGS TODAY:
○ _____

○ _____

○ _____

WHAT I AM READING TODAY:

TOP 3 AREAS THAT NEED CHANGE:
○ _____

○ _____

○ _____

QUESTIONS I HAVE TODAY:
○ _____

○ _____

HOW WOULD YOU RATE THE DAY?
☆ ☆ ☆ ☆ ☆

○ _____

ON WITH YOUR life

DATE: _____

"AHA!" MOMENTS (THINGS I NEVER HEARD
BEFORE OR THAT STRUCK ME AS LIFE-
CHANGING). WHAT DID I LEARN TODAY?
WHAT AM I GRATEFUL FOR TODAY?

ON WITH YOUR life

Dreams, Visions, and Life Goals

Date:

Topic:

Record Special Thoughts on Your Dreams, Visions, and Life Goals
(You can write, doodle, or paste pictures of vision list items.)

DATE: _____

JOURNALING - THOUGHTS, EMOTIONS, AND
SCRIPTURES TO THINK ON. WHAT DID GOD
SAY TO ME TODAY?

_____

_____

_____

_____

_____

_____

_____

_____

_____

_____

TOP 3 GOOD THINGS TODAY:
○ _____

○ _____

○ _____

TOP 3 AREAS THAT NEED CHANGE:
○ _____

○ _____

○ _____

HOW WOULD YOU RATE THE DAY?
☆ ☆ ☆ ☆ ☆

WHAT I AM READING TODAY:

QUESTIONS I HAVE TODAY:
○ _____

○ _____

○ _____

ON
WITH YOUR
life

DATE: _____

"AHA!" MOMENTS (THINGS I NEVER HEARD
BEFORE OR THAT STRUCK ME AS LIFE-
CHANGING). WHAT DID I LEARN TODAY?
WHAT AM I GRATEFUL FOR TODAY?

ON
WITH YOUR
life

_____

_____

_____

_____

_____

_____

_____

_____

_____

_____

_____

_____

_____

_____

_____

_____

_____

_____

_____

_____

_____

_____

Dreams, Visions, and Life Goals

Date:

Topic:

Record Special Thoughts on Your Dreams, Visions, and Life Goals
(You can write, doodle, or paste pictures of vision list items.)

DATE: _____

JOURNALING - THOUGHTS, EMOTIONS, AND
SCRIPTURES TO THINK ON. WHAT DID GOD
SAY TO ME TODAY?

_____

_____

_____

_____

_____

_____

_____

_____

_____

_____

ON WITH YOUR *life*

TOP 3 GOOD THINGS TODAY:
- ○ _____
- ○ _____
- ○ _____

WHAT I AM READING TODAY:

TOP 3 AREAS THAT NEED CHANGE:
- ○ _____
- ○ _____
- ○ _____

QUESTIONS I HAVE TODAY:
- ○ _____
- ○ _____
- ○ _____

HOW WOULD YOU RATE THE DAY?
☆ ☆ ☆ ☆ ☆

DATE: _____

"AHA!" MOMENTS (THINGS I NEVER HEARD
BEFORE OR THAT STRUCK ME AS LIFE-
CHANGING). WHAT DID I LEARN TODAY?
WHAT AM I GRATEFUL FOR TODAY?

ON
WITH YOUR
life

_____
_____
_____
_____
_____
_____
_____
_____
_____
_____
_____
_____
_____
_____
_____
_____
_____
_____
_____
_____
_____
_____

Dreams, Visions, and Life Goals

Date:

Topic:

Record Special Thoughts on Your Dreams, Visions, and Life Goals
(You can write, doodle, or paste pictures of vision list items.)

DATE: _____

JOURNALING - THOUGHTS, EMOTIONS, AND
SCRIPTURES TO THINK ON. WHAT DID GOD
SAY TO ME TODAY? _____

_____

_____

_____

_____

_____

_____

_____

_____

_____

_____

ON
WITH YOUR
life

TOP 3 GOOD THINGS TODAY: _____
○ _____
○ _____
○ _____

WHAT I AM READING TODAY: _____

TOP 3 AREAS THAT NEED CHANGE:
○ _____
○ _____
○ _____

QUESTIONS I HAVE TODAY: _____
○ _____

HOW WOULD YOU RATE THE DAY?
☆ ☆ ☆ ☆ ☆
○ _____
○ _____

DATE: _____

"AHA!" MOMENTS (THINGS I NEVER HEARD BEFORE OR THAT STRUCK ME AS LIFE-CHANGING). WHAT DID I LEARN TODAY? WHAT AM I GRATEFUL FOR TODAY?

ON WITH YOUR *life*

_____

_____

_____

_____

_____

_____

_____

_____

_____

_____

_____

_____

_____

_____

_____

_____

_____

_____

_____

_____

_____

_____

Dreams, Visions, and Life Goals

Date:

Topic:

Record Special Thoughts on Your Dreams, Visions, and Life Goals
(You can write, doodle, or paste pictures of vision list items.)

DATE: _____

JOURNALING - THOUGHTS, EMOTIONS, AND
SCRIPTURES TO THINK ON. WHAT DID GOD
SAY TO ME TODAY? _____

_____

_____

_____

_____

_____

_____

_____

_____

_____

TOP 3 GOOD THINGS TODAY:
○ _____
○ _____
○ _____

WHAT I AM READING TODAY:

TOP 3 AREAS THAT NEED CHANGE:
○ _____
○ _____
○ _____

QUESTIONS I HAVE TODAY:
○ _____
○ _____

HOW WOULD YOU RATE THE DAY?
☆ ☆ ☆ ☆ ☆
○ _____

ON WITH YOUR life

DATE: _____

"AHA!" MOMENTS (THINGS I NEVER HEARD
BEFORE OR THAT STRUCK ME AS LIFE-
CHANGING). WHAT DID I LEARN TODAY?
WHAT AM I GRATEFUL FOR TODAY?

ON
WITH YOUR
life

_____

_____

_____

_____

_____

_____

_____

_____

_____

_____

_____

_____

_____

_____

_____

_____

_____

_____

_____

_____

_____

_____

Dreams, Visions, and Life Goals

Date:

Topic:

Record Special Thoughts on Your Dreams, Visions, and Life Goals
(You can write, doodle, or paste pictures of vision list items.)

DATE: _____

JOURNALING - THOUGHTS, EMOTIONS, AND
SCRIPTURES TO THINK ON. WHAT DID GOD
SAY TO ME TODAY?

_____

_____

_____

_____

_____

_____

_____

_____

_____

_____

_____

ON WITH YOUR life

TOP 3 GOOD THINGS TODAY:

○ _____

○ _____

○ _____

WHAT I AM READING TODAY:
_____

TOP 3 AREAS THAT NEED CHANGE:

○ _____

○ _____

○ _____

QUESTIONS I HAVE TODAY:

○ _____

○ _____

HOW WOULD YOU RATE THE DAY?

☆ ☆ ☆ ☆ ☆

○ _____

DATE: _____

"AHA!" MOMENTS (THINGS I NEVER HEARD
BEFORE OR THAT STRUCK ME AS LIFE-
CHANGING). WHAT DID I LEARN TODAY?
WHAT AM I GRATEFUL FOR TODAY?

ON
WITH YOUR
life

_____

_____

_____

_____

_____

_____

_____

_____

_____

_____

_____

_____

_____

_____

_____

_____

_____

_____

_____

_____

_____

_____

Dreams, Visions, and Life Goals

Date:

Topic:

Record Special Thoughts on Your Dreams, Visions, and Life Goals
(You can write, doodle, or paste pictures of vision list items.)

DATE: _____

JOURNALING - THOUGHTS, EMOTIONS, AND
SCRIPTURES TO THINK ON. WHAT DID GOD
SAY TO ME TODAY? _____

_____

_____

_____

_____

_____

_____

_____

_____

_____

TOP 3 GOOD THINGS TODAY:
○ _____
○ _____
○ _____

TOP 3 AREAS THAT NEED CHANGE:
○ _____
○ _____
○ _____

HOW WOULD YOU RATE THE DAY?
☆ ☆ ☆ ☆ ☆

WHAT I AM READING TODAY:

QUESTIONS I HAVE TODAY:
○ _____
○ _____
○ _____

ON
WITH YOUR
life

DATE: _____

"AHA!" MOMENTS (THINGS I NEVER HEARD
BEFORE OR THAT STRUCK ME AS LIFE-
CHANGING). WHAT DID I LEARN TODAY?
WHAT AM I GRATEFUL FOR TODAY?

ON
WITH YOUR
life

_____

_____

_____

_____

_____

_____

_____

_____

_____

_____

_____

_____

_____

_____

_____

_____

_____

_____

_____

_____

_____

_____

Dreams, Visions, and Life Goals

Date:

Topic:

Record Special Thoughts on Your Dreams, Visions, and Life Goals
(You can write, doodle, or paste pictures of vision list items.)

DATE: _____

JOURNALING - THOUGHTS, EMOTIONS, AND
SCRIPTURES TO THINK ON. WHAT DID GOD
SAY TO ME TODAY? _____

_____

_____

_____

_____

_____

_____

_____

_____

_____

_____

TOP 3 GOOD THINGS TODAY:
- ○ _____
- ○ _____
- ○ _____

WHAT I AM READING TODAY:

TOP 3 AREAS THAT NEED CHANGE:
- ○ _____
- ○ _____
- ○ _____

QUESTIONS I HAVE TODAY:
- ○ _____
- ○ _____
- ○ _____

HOW WOULD YOU RATE THE DAY?
☆ ☆ ☆ ☆ ☆

ON WITH YOUR life

DATE: _____

"AHA!" MOMENTS (THINGS I NEVER HEARD
BEFORE OR THAT STRUCK ME AS LIFE-
CHANGING). WHAT DID I LEARN TODAY?
WHAT AM I GRATEFUL FOR TODAY?

ON
WITH YOUR
life

Dreams, Visions, and Life Goals

Date:

Topic:

Record Special Thoughts on Your Dreams, Visions, and Life Goals
(You can write, doodle, or paste pictures of vision list items.)

DATE: _____

JOURNALING - THOUGHTS, EMOTIONS, AND
SCRIPTURES TO THINK ON. WHAT DID GOD
SAY TO ME TODAY? _____

_____

_____

_____

_____

_____

_____

_____

_____

_____

TOP 3 GOOD THINGS TODAY:
○ _____

○ _____

○ _____

WHAT I AM READING TODAY:

TOP 3 AREAS THAT NEED CHANGE:
○ _____

○ _____

○ _____

HOW WOULD YOU RATE THE DAY?
☆ ☆ ☆ ☆ ☆

QUESTIONS I HAVE TODAY:
○ _____

○ _____

○ _____

DATE: _____

"AHA!" MOMENTS (THINGS I NEVER HEARD
BEFORE OR THAT STRUCK ME AS LIFE-
CHANGING). WHAT DID I LEARN TODAY?
WHAT AM I GRATEFUL FOR TODAY?

ON
WITH YOUR
life

_____

_____

_____

_____

_____

_____

_____

_____

_____

_____

_____

_____

_____

_____

_____

_____

_____

_____

_____

_____

_____

_____

Dreams, Visions, and Life Goals

Date:

Topic:

Record Special Thoughts on Your Dreams, Visions, and Life Goals
(You can write, doodle, or paste pictures of vision list items.)

DATE: _____

JOURNALING - THOUGHTS, EMOTIONS, AND
SCRIPTURES TO THINK ON. WHAT DID GOD
SAY TO ME TODAY?

_____

_____

_____

_____

_____

_____

_____

_____

_____

_____

_____

TOP 3 GOOD THINGS TODAY:
○ _____

○ _____

○ _____

TOP 3 AREAS THAT NEED CHANGE:
○ _____

○ _____

○ _____

HOW WOULD YOU RATE THE DAY?
☆ ☆ ☆ ☆ ☆

WHAT I AM READING TODAY:

QUESTIONS I HAVE TODAY:
○ _____

○ _____

○ _____

DATE: _____

"AHA!" MOMENTS (THINGS I NEVER HEARD
BEFORE OR THAT STRUCK ME AS LIFE-
CHANGING). WHAT DID I LEARN TODAY?
WHAT AM I GRATEFUL FOR TODAY?

**ON
WITH YOUR
life**

_____

_____

_____

_____

_____

_____

_____

_____

_____

_____

_____

_____

_____

_____

_____

_____

_____

_____

_____

_____

_____

_____

Dreams, Visions, and Life Goals

Date:

Topic:

Record Special Thoughts on Your Dreams, Visions, and Life Goals
(You can write, doodle, or paste pictures of vision list items.)

DATE: _____

JOURNALING - THOUGHTS, EMOTIONS, AND
SCRIPTURES TO THINK ON. WHAT DID GOD
SAY TO ME TODAY? _____

_____

_____

_____

_____

_____

_____

_____

_____

_____

_____

ON WITH YOUR life

TOP 3 GOOD THINGS TODAY:
- ○ _____
- ○ _____
- ○ _____

TOP 3 AREAS THAT NEED CHANGE:
- ○ _____
- ○ _____
- ○ _____

HOW WOULD YOU RATE THE DAY?
☆ ☆ ☆ ☆ ☆

WHAT I AM READING TODAY:

QUESTIONS I HAVE TODAY:
- ○ _____
- ○ _____
- ○ _____

DATE: _____

"AHA!" MOMENTS (THINGS I NEVER HEARD
BEFORE OR THAT STRUCK ME AS LIFE-
CHANGING). WHAT DID I LEARN TODAY?
WHAT AM I GRATEFUL FOR TODAY?

_____
_____
_____
_____
_____
_____
_____
_____
_____
_____
_____
_____
_____
_____
_____
_____
_____
_____
_____
_____
_____
_____
_____
_____
_____

Dreams, Visions, and Life Goals

Date:

Topic:

Record Special Thoughts on Your Dreams, Visions, and Life Goals
(You can write, doodle, or paste pictures of vision list items.)

DATE: _____

JOURNALING - THOUGHTS, EMOTIONS, AND
SCRIPTURES TO THINK ON. WHAT DID GOD
SAY TO ME TODAY? _____

_____

_____

_____

_____

_____

_____

_____

_____

_____

TOP 3 GOOD THINGS TODAY: _____

○ _____

○ _____

○ _____

WHAT I AM READING TODAY: _____

TOP 3 AREAS THAT NEED CHANGE:

○ _____

○ _____

○ _____

QUESTIONS I HAVE TODAY: _____

○ _____

○ _____

HOW WOULD YOU RATE THE DAY?

☆ ☆ ☆ ☆ ☆

○ _____

DATE: _____

"AHA!" MOMENTS (THINGS I NEVER HEARD
BEFORE OR THAT STRUCK ME AS LIFE-
CHANGING). WHAT DID I LEARN TODAY?
WHAT AM I GRATEFUL FOR TODAY?

ON
WITH YOUR
life

_____

_____

_____

_____

_____

_____

_____

_____

_____

_____

_____

_____

_____

_____

_____

_____

_____

_____

_____

_____

_____

Dreams, Visions, and Life Goals

Date:

Topic:

Record Special Thoughts on Your Dreams, Visions, and Life Goals
(You can write, doodle, or paste pictures of vision list items.)

DATE: _____

JOURNALING - THOUGHTS, EMOTIONS, AND
SCRIPTURES TO THINK ON. WHAT DID GOD
SAY TO ME TODAY? _____

_____

_____

_____

_____

_____

_____

_____

_____

_____

TOP 3 GOOD THINGS TODAY: _____

○ _____

○ _____

○ _____

WHAT I AM READING TODAY: _____

TOP 3 AREAS THAT NEED CHANGE:

○ _____

○ _____

○ _____

QUESTIONS I HAVE TODAY: _____

○ _____

HOW WOULD YOU RATE THE DAY?

☆ ☆ ☆ ☆ ☆

○ _____

○ _____

DATE: _____

"AHA!" MOMENTS (THINGS I NEVER HEARD
BEFORE OR THAT STRUCK ME AS LIFE-
CHANGING). WHAT DID I LEARN TODAY?
WHAT AM I GRATEFUL FOR TODAY?

ON
WITH YOUR
life

_____

_____

_____

_____

_____

_____

_____

_____

_____

_____

_____

_____

_____

_____

_____

_____

_____

_____

_____

_____

_____

Dreams, Visions, and Life Goals

Date:

Topic:

Record Special Thoughts on Your Dreams, Visions, and Life Goals
(You can write, doodle, or paste pictures of vision list items.)

DATE: _____

JOURNALING - THOUGHTS, EMOTIONS, AND
SCRIPTURES TO THINK ON. WHAT DID GOD
SAY TO ME TODAY? _____

_____

_____

_____

_____

_____

_____

_____

_____

_____

ON
WITH YOUR
life

TOP 3 GOOD THINGS TODAY:
○ _____
○ _____
○ _____

TOP 3 AREAS THAT NEED CHANGE:
○ _____
○ _____
○ _____

HOW WOULD YOU RATE THE DAY?
☆ ☆ ☆ ☆ ☆

WHAT I AM READING TODAY:

QUESTIONS I HAVE TODAY:
○ _____
○ _____
○ _____

DATE: _____

"AHA!" MOMENTS (THINGS I NEVER HEARD
BEFORE OR THAT STRUCK ME AS LIFE-
CHANGING). WHAT DID I LEARN TODAY?
WHAT AM I GRATEFUL FOR TODAY?

ON
WITH YOUR
life

Dreams, Visions, and Life Goals

Date:

Topic:

Record Special Thoughts on Your Dreams, Visions, and Life Goals
(You can write, doodle, or paste pictures of vision list items.)

DATE: _____

JOURNALING - THOUGHTS, EMOTIONS, AND
SCRIPTURES TO THINK ON. WHAT DID GOD
SAY TO ME TODAY? _____

_____

_____

_____

_____

_____

_____

_____

_____

_____

_____

ON WITH YOUR life

TOP 3 GOOD THINGS TODAY: _____

○ _____
○ _____
○ _____

TOP 3 AREAS THAT NEED CHANGE:

○ _____
○ _____
○ _____

HOW WOULD YOU RATE THE DAY?

☆ ☆ ☆ ☆ ☆

WHAT I AM READING TODAY: _____

QUESTIONS I HAVE TODAY: _____

○ _____
○ _____
○ _____

DATE: _____

"AHA!" MOMENTS (THINGS I NEVER HEARD
BEFORE OR THAT STRUCK ME AS LIFE-
CHANGING). WHAT DID I LEARN TODAY?
WHAT AM I GRATEFUL FOR TODAY?

ON
WITH YOUR
life

_____

_____

_____

_____

_____

_____

_____

_____

_____

_____

_____

_____

_____

_____

_____

_____

_____

_____

_____

_____

_____

_____

_____

_____

Dreams, Visions, and Life Goals

Date:

Topic:

Record Special Thoughts on Your Dreams, Visions, and Life Goals
(You can write, doodle, or paste pictures of vision list items.)

DATE: _____

JOURNALING - THOUGHTS, EMOTIONS, AND
SCRIPTURES TO THINK ON. WHAT DID GOD
SAY TO ME TODAY? _____

_____

_____
_____
_____
_____
_____
_____
_____
_____
_____

ON
WITH YOUR
life

TOP 3 GOOD THINGS TODAY: _____
○ _____
○ _____
○ _____

WHAT I AM READING TODAY: _____

TOP 3 AREAS THAT NEED CHANGE: _____
○ _____
○ _____
○ _____

QUESTIONS I HAVE TODAY: _____
○ _____

HOW WOULD YOU RATE THE DAY?
☆ ☆ ☆ ☆ ☆
○ _____
○ _____

DATE: _____

"AHA!" MOMENTS (THINGS I NEVER HEARD
BEFORE OR THAT STRUCK ME AS LIFE-
CHANGING). WHAT DID I LEARN TODAY?
WHAT AM I GRATEFUL FOR TODAY?

ON
WITH YOUR
life

Dreams, Visions, and Life Goals

Date:

Topic:

Record Special Thoughts on Your Dreams, Visions, and Life Goals
(You can write, doodle, or paste pictures of vision list items.)

Meet the Author:
Dana Marie Ecklund

Author. Speaker. Teacher. Businesswoman. Friend. Whatever role or venue you meet her in, you will soon discover that Dana's biggest desire is to lead people to Jesus and help them see who they are as born-again believers. She is a cheerleader at heart and loves seeing people get off circumstantial merry-go-rounds and on to the path God has for them in this life.

Here's a lady who has gone through numerous trials and tribulations and has remained faithful, not just months or weeks, but for years. Her faith has been displayed and defined throughout her 38 years of marriage as she and her husband raised four children amidst impossible situations. Her various life experiences, which took her on one merry-go-round after another, cover the following areas and more: religious legalism, sexual identity crises, pornography, sexual abuse, family members who struggled with substance abuse lifestyles (including prison and rehab time), her own marriage struggles, children with major health diagnoses, work, school, and more.

Through all of these things, Dana has proven that she can recognize merry-go-rounds and is not afraid to get off and go forward. No matter the circumstances or situations she faced, she never quit believing God and His Word. She held to the Word of God. It has been her Rock. It is evident that her foundation, who is the Lord Jesus Christ, is strong! This is who she is, and her victories are fully displayed in her life.

In 2017, Dana and her husband, David, jumped off the merry-go-round of frustration caused by not moving forward into their hearts' desires. As they finally stepped out to follow God's plan for their lives together, they attended Charis Bible College in Woodland Park, CO, on campus for the next three years. Dana graduated her third year from the Charis Business School, and David from the Charis Practical Government School, in May 2020. Determined to keep moving forward, she is building the business God dropped in her heart in 2015. She is also helping her husband express his God-given passions through his Good News teachings of the true Gospel of Jesus Christ and the Church's role in culture.

Dana and David Ecklund began their marriage in Southern California in 1983. They moved to raise their family in the mid-west and are now back in Southern California. Dana is a mother of three daughters, one son, and a grandmother of seven so far.

To invite Dana Marie Ecklund to speak,
to find additional products and motivational tools, or
to purchase additional copies, please visit :

OnWithYourLife.com